Gardening
WITH THE EXPERTS

BULBS

Gardening WITH THE EXPERTS

BULBS

MARY MOODY

HARLAXTON
PUBLISHING

Cover: *Glorious red **Tulipa** (tulips)*.

Published by Harlaxton Publishing Ltd
2 Avenue Road, Grantham, Lincolnshire, NG31 6TA, United Kingdom.
A Member of the Weldon International Group of Companies.

First published in 1992.
Reprinted 1993

Publishing Manager: Robin Burgess
Project Coordinator: Mary Moody
Editor: Christine Mackinnon
Illustrator: Kathie Baxter Smith
Designed & produced for the publisher by Phillip Mathews Publishers
Produced in Singapore by Imago

British Library Cataloguing-in-Publication data.
A catalogue record for this book is available from the British Library.
Title: Gardening with the Experts: Bulbs
ISBN:1 85837 034 5

CONTENTS

INTRODUCTION

The terms 'bulb' is loosely used to cover a wide range of plants such as corms, tubers and rhizomes. All of these hold their storage organs beneath the ground in one form or another.

Bulbs can be incorporated into the garden by naturalising them throughout lawns or including them as part of an herbaceous border, garden bed or rockery. They can be grown successfully in many climates and soil conditions, and there are species suited to every region, no matter how harsh the climate. Really spectacular results can be achieved by enriching the soil, feeding, and watering with care; however, there are many hardy varieties which manage to thrive in low maintenance landscapes with just a minimum of care and attention. Some multiply quickly year after year and can be lifted, divided and replanted to fill every garden corner.

TYPES OF BULBS

Bulbs can be divided into four main categories, differing in their structure beneath the ground as well as in their foliage and flower types.

Bulbs: Classified as modified leaves which have become swollen food-storage scales, bulbs have a distinct basal disc, from which the roots emerge, and an oval or pear-shaped outline e.g. daffodils, tulips.

Rhizomes: Stems which grow either at ground level or just beneath ground level, spreading horizontally. Rhizomes have foliage that emerges from the top of these horizontal stems, while the root system develops underneath e.g. canna lily.

Corms: Modified stems, generally without regular layers or scales, although there is a protective outer skin. Corms are solid inside, not layered like bulbs e.g. gladioli.

Tubers: These are divided into two groups: stem tubers which generally grow at ground level and are solid and fleshy, with shoots emerging from the top and roots going into the ground from the base e.g. tuberous rooted begonias and cyclamens; root tubers which grow below ground with shoots arising from a piece of the stem at the crown e.g. dahlias.

Bulbs can be grown in conjunction with many other species. Some of the most spectacular displays are created when bulbs are overplanted with annuals and the bulbs simply emerge through the young plants. The annuals can be timed to flower simultaneously with the bulbs, or to follow the bulbs so that the garden bed has colour over a long period. In fact it is a good idea to follow bulbs with a planting of annuals, as the garden can look rather bare during

*Opposite: Tall slender stems of the **Iris** species.*

Pale yellow tulips at their most dramatic in a massed planting.

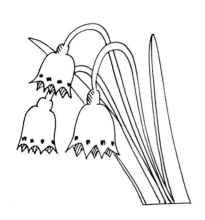

Leucojum (*snowflake*) *appear in late winter.*

the period when the bulbs' foliage is wilting after flowering.

The wilting foliage must never be cut back but allowed to die back naturally to provide a good storehouse of nutrients for the following season.

If you decide to grow bulbs beneath annuals, keep in mind, that the demand for feeding will be quite high since both species will require sufficient nutrients for healthy, productive growth.

HEALTHY SOIL FOR BULBS

Bulbs require moderately rich and well-drained soil, and it is important to provide these growing conditions to achieve good results. As bulbs contain a storehouse of nutrients they will usually flower well the first year, even in poor soil; however, if this is the case subsequent flowering will be of a low standard.

For maximum flowering the ground should be well prepared prior to planting. The most effective way of creating a good growing environment is to add plenty of organic soil builders in the form of manures and composts.

Soil builders add valuable nutrients to the soil, they also improve the texture, structure and soil drainage qualities.

USEFUL SOIL ADDITIVES

Compost: Good gardeners consistently produce a supply of home-made compost to add to garden beds as a mulch. Have three heaps going at once – one to use, one breaking down, one being built. Mushroom compost adds texture to the soil, although it lacks many basic nutrients.

Manures: Cow, horse, sheep and poultry manures are the oldest and most accepted soil builders used in both agriculture and domestic landscaping. They improve soil

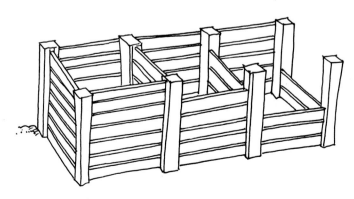

A supply of compost can be made using three bins: one in use; one decomposing; one being built.

*Tulips backed by **Agapanthus** and framed with a border of low-growing **Viola**.*

texture and drainage, to provide a good supply of nutrients for the plants. Never use fresh manures, always allow them to rot well or sensitive plants may be damaged.

Seaweed: Gardeners living near the sea can bring home seaweed to add to the garden. Rinse the salt away thoroughly and add chopped weed to the compost or use it directly in the ground.

HOW TO MAKE COMPOST

Home-made compost is a valuable soil additive which can be easily prepared, even in a small garden. Where ground space is limited invest in a compost bin or tumbler which can be easily stored in a corner out of the way.

Compost is made by combining a range of organic materials and ensuring that they have both moisture and air circulation to hasten decomposition. A well-made compost should be ready for spreading on the garden after eight to twelve weeks. During this time tremendous heat should have generated on the inside of the heap reducing the organic materials into light, friable humus (soil).

When using a compost tumbler, the turning action aerates the compost and hastens decomposition. However water must be added regularly to keep this process going.

A heap made on the ground will require regular turning with a fork to allow air to penetrate. It should also be watered weekly to maintain the breaking down process.

Suitable ingredients for a healthy compost heap include leaves, grass clippings, straw, kitchen scraps, shredded bark, manures and wood ashes.

Opposite: In most climates tulip bulbs must be lifted annually after flowering.

PLANTING AND PROPAGATION

When choosing bulbs for the garden, always look for the healthiest and strongest specimens. Obviously this is impossible when buying through mail order, however most nurseries are reputable and only send out their best and healthiest stock.

Always look closely for firm bulbs, corms or tubers, which seem solid and heavy for their size. With bulbs and corms, the larger and heavier the better in terms of flowering potential.

When selecting tubers only look for healthy specimens, as size is not as important. Check the outer skin of the bulb and choose those with the least damage.

Bulbs are planted at twice their depth.

Do not choose bulbs that are obviously shrivelled, or have any soft spots, in particular around the base or the neck. Reject bulbs with any sign of mould, no matter how slight, and look carefully to ensure there are no insects that could weaken or destroy them.

PLANTING TIPS
Bulbs will generally survive and flower well, even when they are poorly planted. They can survive being planted upside down, although this is not recommended. Remember that the soil should have been enriched with plenty of organic matter prior to planting, but that there is no need to incorporate specific fertiliser into the planting hole, as bulbs contain their own storehouse of nutrients for the first flowering season. Subsequently they will require annual fertilising to maintain the best results.

STEP-BY-STEP
1. The general rule is that bulbs need to be planted at twice their depth. i.e. a 2cm (1/2 in) tall bulb needs to be planted at a depth of 4cm (1 in). If soil drainage is poor, some sand in the base of the planting hole will create a better growing environment.
2. A close look at the bulb will determine which way to plant it. Generally the

base is flatter than the top, which
should have a slight point. With more
rounded bulbs, like gladiolus, it can be
hard to tell unless there is some
evidence of a shoot.

3. Excavate a hole, allowing depth for
   sand if it is required.
4. Position a slender stick in the hole
   beside the planted bulbs. This marker
   will act as a reminder not to dig it up
   later by accident!
5. Position the bulb, or bulbs in the hole.
   Remember that three or more planted
   together creates a better clumped effect.
6. Replace soil around the bulb, pressing
   down firmly to ensure that there are no
   air pockets, but take care not to apply
   too much pressure.
7. Avoid overwatering since bulbs are
   susceptible to fungal disease and will rot
   in the ground if too much moisture
   surrounds them.

*Sand can be added to the base of the hole to
improve drainage if necessary.*

BULB PROPAGATION

Most bulbs, tubers and corms can be easily
propagated by lifting and dividing them
every few years. In fact most will benefit
from being divided occasionally as flower
production is reduced if they are left
undisturbed indefinitely.

The way in which bulbs are propagated
depends on their structure. True bulbs
produce small offsets which grow around
the base of the mature bulb, then these in
turn will grow into mature bulbs when
separated from the parent bulb.

Use a fork to lift the bulbs and gently
break off the small bulbs – sometimes they
just fall off naturally when being lifted.

The immature bulbs should be re-planted
in a special area of the garden, where they
will follow the normal growth cycle for two
years until ready to flower. At this stage

they can be transplanted back into the
main garden.

Corms produce cormlets around the edge
of the base of the mature corm every
season. When propagating, lift the corms
and gently pull away the cormlets, replanting the mature corm. There may be
evidence of a previous corm which has
withered and died and this should be
pulled away and discarded. The cormlets
can be grown for one season in a separate
bed, then transplanted into the garden
when they are ready to flower.

Rhizomes and tubers are propagated by
actually cutting the mature stock with a
clean sharp knife. Always ensure that each
cut section has either an eye or a section of
stem to ensure it will grow. Replant this
immediately where the plant is to grow.

How popular bulbs are propagated:
Narcissus: Daffodils and jonquils should
be lifted every three or four years. Wait
until all the foliage has completely died
back, then lift with care using a spade or

fork. The mother bulb will be surrounded by small bulbs which should break away with no problems. Store them in a cool, dark place for replanting in autumn.

Dahlias: During late autumn as the dahlia foliage begins to brown, lift them for storing and replanting the following spring. This should be done every year. Use a clean, sharp knife to cut the tubers, making sure that each has a section of the crown and at least one dormant eye.

Iris: Rhizomes like iris need to be divided every three years or they will show signs of overcrowding. Use a fork to lift out the root mass in autumn, then cut off the rhizomes growing on the outer edge using a sharp, clean knife. Also the foliage should be cut back to about half its size to compensate. Replant immediately.

Lilies: To propagate lilies, lift the bulbs every three years and remove the old stems. Carefully separate the bulbs, including the small bulblets and offsets, and replant immediately.

Gladiolus: As corms, gladiolus should be lifted every few years. If several corms have formed they can be separated, or if there is just one large corm it can be cut in half and replanted. Always remember to use a clean, sharp knife.

Tuberous begonias: Begonias also need to be cut when new shoots appear on the tubers. Use a clean knife and cut down through the tuber, making sure that each section has an eye. Place the tubers to dry for a few days in a cool, dark and dry location before replanting.

Tulips: Tulips will not continue to flower year after year unless lifted and stored in a cool, dry place until autumn when they should be planted where they are to grow. Tulips produce offsets, in the same way as daffodils, so these can be replanted into a separate bed and left alone for a few seasons until they are ready to flower.

After foliage has died back bulbs can be lifted and stored in a dry, dark place for the following season.

*Opposite: **Narcissus** (daffodils) interplanted with annuals, shrubs and perennials.*
*Overleaf: Brilliant yellow trumpet flowers of **Narcissus** (daffodils) in early spring.*

GENERAL MAINTENANCE

All gardens require basic maintenance to produce the best results. There are various routine chores that must be attended to, including mulching, weeding, watering and feeding.

MULCHING

Mulching of the soil on top of bulbs will not prevent them from emerging. It will help reduce garden maintenance in a variety of ways:

1. Mulch stops weeds from emerging.
2. Mulch keeps the soil moist between waterings and prevents the surface from drying out.
3. Mulch improves soil texture by keeping it lightly moist.
4. When organic mulch is used a steady stream of nutrients is supplied to the plant roots.
5. As the mulch breaks down it builds the soil into rich, friable humus.

With bulbs, the best time to mulch is after planting repeated again when the first shoots appear. A good layer of manure mulch can be applied when the bulbs have died back, which will help to feed them the following season. The best mulches are compost, animal manures, bark chips, leaves or leaf mulch.

WEEDING

Bulbs do not easily compete with weed growth which depletes the soil of moisture

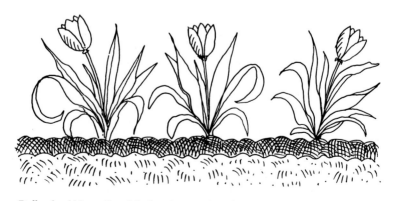

Bulbs should be well mulched with organic matter to keep weed growth down.

Bulbs grow well in rich, moist soil with good drainage.

and nutrients. If the area around bulbs is well mulched, weeding will be less of a problem. If, however, weeds persist, water the ground several hours before weeding to make the task easier and less traumatic on the bulbs. If the ground is lightly moistened, weeds should lift out easily.

Avoid heavy cultivation which will disturb bulb growth and possibly damage new shoots.

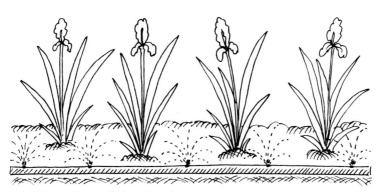

Water bulbs regularly in hot, dry weather, taking care not to overwater.

*Hardy bulbs like **Endymion** (bluebells) can be grown beneath deciduous trees with great success.*

Bulbs can be fed with a formulated bulb food that will supply the correct balance of nutrients.

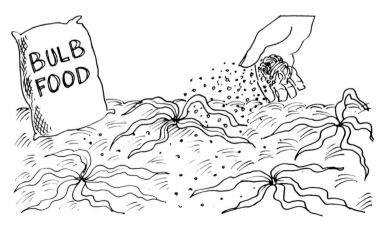

Feed bulbs after flowering, when the foliage is dying back.

WATERING

Bulbs should not be overwatered although regular moisture is required for healthy growth. Providing the soil has good drainage qualities, overwatering should not be a problem. However, if the soil is inclined to be boggy, attempt to improve the texture by adding plenty of compost or manures. The amount of watering the garden requires depends on the type of soil, the style of garden and the general climate (natural rainfall).

When to water: During warm or hot weather it is best to water either early in the morning or early in the evening. Wait until direct sun has moved from the garden before turning your sprinkler on. In winter, in cold climates, if watering is needed, choose mid-morning rather than late afternoon. The risk of late watering is that overnight cold may freeze remaining water trapped on foliage, which can then damage certain species.

FEEDING

The bulbous part of the plant – either rhizome, tuber, corm or bulb – is the nutrient storehouse. When bulbs are first bought they should contain sufficient nutrients for the first year's growth. If the foliage is then allowed to yellow, wither and die, there will be sufficient nutrients stored for the following season. For really good results, consider the following:

Enrich the soil: always incorporate plenty of rich organic matter into the ground prior to planting your bulb stock. This also helps to improve drainage and supplies additional nutrients to the growing plants. If the soil is rich, no extra fertiliser should be required during the first growing season.

Avoid nitrogen-rich fertilisers: too much nitrogen will encourage rapid foliage growth, often at the expense of flower production. Avoid poultry manure and use horse or cow manure as a soil builder.

Mulch: after the foliage has died down mulch the ground thoroughly with a mixture of compost and well-rotted manures. This will keep weeds down as well as supplying nutrients.

Bulb food: there are several brands of specially formulated bulb food that give excellent results. These can be used as a top-dressing during the period when the foliage is dying back, and applied again, very early in the growing season when the flowers are beginning to form.

Liquid fertiliser: again make sure the liquid formula is balanced and not too high in nitrogen. Apply a weak solution once a fortnight during the main growing period.

Overleaf: Tulips are suited to cold climates and require rich, moist and well-drained soil.

AN ALPHABET OF BULBS

Agapanthus (African lily): A native of
South Africa, this plant forms a clump of
deep green strap-like leaves, from which
emerge tall stalks topped by circular
flowerheads. Relatively hardy, they thrive
in any fertile, well-drained soil; choose a
sunny and sheltered position especially in
cooler climates. Miniature forms are
available. Colours range from white, to
various shades of mauve and blue. Propagate by division of clumps, or from seed.

Allium (onion, garlic): A delightful bulb
for the cottage garden, with tall slender
stems and dramatic flowerheads. Quite easy
to grow, *Allium* species like moderately rich
and well-drained soil and should be
positioned in full sun. Plant bulbs in late
autumn or spring and mulch with well-
rotted animal manure to produce good
foliage and flowers. Each year the bulbs can
be lifted and divided in autumn. The
healthiest bulbs can then be replanted to
form new clumps.

Amaryllis belladonna (naked lady,
belladonna lily): A native of South Africa,
each stem of this beautiful bulb has a
profusion of trumpet-shaped, rose-red
flowers, blooming from summer through to
autumn. Plant in full sun in deep, rich soil,
and ensure that the position is sheltered for
repeated good displays season after season.
Useful as a border along a driveway, or
against a warm, sunny wall.

Anemone (windflower): *Anemones* require
rich, well-drained and lightly moist (not
wet) soil, they will only thrive if good

*Pretty **Agapanthus** is easy to grow in most soils and conditions.*

Colourful **Anemone** *(windflower).*

growing conditions are provided. For spring flowering, plant in early winter, providing the ground is not too cold. A warm, sheltered position will give good results.

Babania (baboon flower): A native of South Africa, *babania* is a member of the iris family with strap-like foliage and funnel shaped flowers. There are many hybrids with colours ranging from white through yellow, cream, red and mauve. For good results plant corms in full sun in a moderately rich and well-drained soil. Suits indoor pot cultivation in cool regions.

Begonia: *Begonias* have marvellous foliage and attractive, sometimes showy flowers. *Begonias* need soil rich in organic matter, and regular watering is required in summer, especially when the plants are flowering. However, take care not to waterlog the soil. Choose a warm, sheltered and semi-shaded position, and in winter keep the soil rather dry – this applies to both potted and garden begonias.

Brodiaea x tubergenii: Native to the Americas, these delicate bulbs are best when planted in dense groups to give a good display. Flowers range through various blues to purple, and some are tinged with orange. Relatively hardy, they can survive in any average garden providing a well-drained and sunny position, preferably with the protection of a south wall. Allow them to multiply year after year – they require very little attention once established. Suited to greenhouse cultivation in cold regions.

Canna (Indian shot): *Canna* forms a clump of dark green foliage with tall spikes of elegant flowers in the orange/red/yellow colour range. Enrich the soil with plenty of

Overleaf: **Crocus** *grow well in pots.*

27

organic matter prior to planting out in a sunny, sheltered position in early summer. Bring plants under cover before autumn frosts begin.

Cardiocrinum giganteum (giant lily): This plant grows more than 2 metres (6ft) in height, with heart-shaped foliage and tall stems of drooping white trumpet flowers in summer. It must have the right growing conditions, soil must be rich and moist, although good drainage is important. Keep a good water supply and mulch with well-rotted manure or compost every spring. Being monocarpic, plants die after flowering, leaving offset bulbs to reach flowering size after 3 to 5 years.

Chionodoxa (glory of the snow): Charming small bulbs which start flowering in late winter and continue through to mid-spring. They are best positioned in full sun or semi-shade, they look effective when scattered in drifts beneath deciduous trees. Add organic matter to the soil before planting, and ensure adequate drainage. Cultivate by lifting and separating bulbs.

Colchicum (autumn crocus): A dramatic burst of colour in autumn, *crocus* grow to 30cm (12in) in height and emerge without foliage. Select a sunny or semi-shaded and sheltered position and ensure the soil is rich and moist before planting in late summer. Ideal as part of a rock garden or as a border plant in the flower garden. To divide the plants lift and move them while in flower and replant immediately.

Crinum (Cape lily): More than 100 species of large, showy bulbs with fragrant flowers in the rose, pink and white colour range. Choose a sunny but sheltered position, and ensure the soil is rich and well-drained. Water well, especially during summer. Only lift every four years, and propagate by gently removing offsets from mature bulbs.

Crocus: Small, hardy bulbs, native of Europe and the Mediterranean, *Crocus* look delightful naturalised in drifts beneath deciduous trees, or as part of a rock garden. Suited to cultivation in a wide range of soils and conditions. Choose a sunny position, and water well but take care not to overwater as they should not be waterlogged. Propagation is from division and replanting of offsets.

Cyclamen: *Cyclamen* have attractive

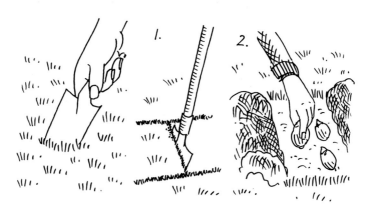

Naturalise bulbs beneath deciduous trees to create a woodland garden.

30

Glorious red and yellow **Canna** *(Indian shot).*

foliage and slender stems with soft flowers in the pink, red and white colour range. They require a warm, sheltered environ-ment with soil that is humus-rich and well drained. Water well, especially in summer, but take care not to overwater! Only use fertiliser sparingly.

Dahlia: These old-fashioned favourites have dramatic flowers in a variety of forms, many are large and colourful. They can be grown in a wide range of soils and condi-tions, large varieties require staking to prevent damage when the flowers emerge.

Endymion (bluebell): Very easy to grow in a wide range of soils and conditions, bluebells should be positioned in a location where they cannot overtake or smother other species. They look effective natural-ised beneath deciduous trees, and are good in shady places where little else will grow. Plant in moderately rich and well-drained

soil. Clumps can be lifted and divided after the foliage dies back.

Eranthis (winter aconite): A low-growing tuber that spreads like a groundcover with flowers of vivid yellow. Although difficult to establish, once they find a suitable environment they should thrive providing soil is rich and moist. Water regularly, especially during warm summer weather. Propagation is from offsets of the tubers which require soaking overnight in water prior to planting.

Erythronium: A member of the lily family, there are various foliage and flower forms that thrive in moderately rich, well-drained soil in a semi-shaded situation. Corms should be planted in autumn and should require very little maintenance

Overleaf: Bulbs planted in the lawn must be allowed to die back completely after flowering.

31

apart from watering in summer. Clumps can be divided every three or four years to produce new plants.

Freesia: One of the most prized garden bulbs, *freesias* are available in many flower colours and forms, including some excellent new giant hybrids which are very showy indeed. Valued for their glorious scent, freesias require full sun and light, rich, sandy, well-drained soil with a sheltered site.

Fritillaria: Tall stems topped with spiky leaves and drooping bell-like flowers. Requirements vary according to the species, but in general the soil must be well-drained but moist, a sunny, but sheltered position must be found. Lift, divide and replant every second or third year. Ensure that the bulbs are replanted immediately as they dry out rapidly.

Galanthus (snowdrop): Snowdrops have deep green foliage and tall flower spikes topped by delicate white bell- flowers. Flowering in late winter and early spring, they require deep, rich, moist soil, and either full sun or semi-shaded conditions to produce a good display. Bulbs can be lifted and divided every few years.

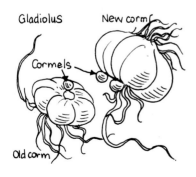

Freesias *are available in many varieties.*

Galtonia candicans (summer hyacinth): A summer-flowering bulb with fragrant white bellflowers on a tall, slender stem. *Galtonia* requires an open, sunny position with protection from strong winds, and a moist, well- drained soil. Plant bulbs in clumps of three or five, and mulch well with organic matter during winter. Propagate every four years by lifting the offsets from the bulbs towards late summer.

Gladiolus (sword lily): Dramatic flowering corms with sword-like foliage and tall flower spikes. There are many hybrid forms, from miniature to giant varieties, in a wide range of colours from creamy white through salmon, orange, pink, violet-blue to deep scarlet. *Gladioli* like a sunny aspect and a well-drained soil that has been enriched with plenty of organic matter.

Gloriosa (climbing lily): This spectacular climbing lily has bright yellow and red flame-like petals which turn to orange and claret as the flower matures. A most unusual and exotic greenhouse plant, except in the mildest and most sheltered regions, where it maybe planted out early summer for late summer flowering. It climbs on tendrils and can be trained on a wall or trellis. Conditions must be warm and moist with protection from wind.

Hemerocallis (day lily): A bulb that forms a dense clump of slender leaves and tall stalks of dramatic flowers which can be orange, yellow, lavender, purple, red, maroon, bronze, pink, cream or off-white in colour. A well-drained soil, enriched with organic matter, will give good results. Divide in autumn when clumps become crowded, usually after three to six years.

Hippeastrum (*Amaryllis*): A native of South America, with strap-like leaves and tall stems that carry three or four showy trumpet flowers. Growing to about 1 metre

*Above: Grow bulbs in terracotta pots.   Below: Brilliant purple-blue **Muscari** (grape hyacinth).*

Hyacinth can be grown successfully in containers as well as in the ground.

fragrance as well as attractive blooms. Originally from the Mediterranean, some of the larger species can reach 45cm (18in) in height, with waxy bell-shaped flowers during late winter and spring. Flower colours range from white through blue, to purple, red, pink, salmon, buff, yellow and pale cream.

Potted, forced bulbs can be planted out during spring to recover and continue flowering. Left undisturbed they will flower year after year.

Good drainage is essential for success, and bulbs should be planted in clumps or *en masse* for the best effect.

Ipheion (Triteleia, spring star flower): A spring and summer flowering bulb, growing to 20cm (8in) in height with delightful blue or white flowers tinged with blue. Will thrive in sun or partial shade in moderately rich, well-drained soil. Clumps should be left undisturbed for several years until well established.

(3ft) the right conditions, flowers can be multi-coloured, red, orange, pink or white. Rich, moist and well-drained soil conditions are essential for success. Needs indoor or greenhouse cultivation in cool areas.

Hyacinthus (hyacinth): A popular group of bulbs, valued for their beautiful scented

Hemerocallis (day lily) has tall slender stems and showy flowers.

*Pretty **Ipheion** forms a carpet of flowers.*

Iris: There are many species and varieties of *iris* in two forms, rhizome and true bulb. They can be seen in flower over most of the year, depending on the variety and when it was planted. Colours cover the entire spectrum, except for true red. There are also many multicoloured varieties. All *irises* thrive in full sun in soil that has been well enriched with organic matter, and has good drainage.

Ixia (African corn lily): A native of South Africa, it can survive outdoors in milder regions, or potted, positioned with a sunny aspect. A warm climate corm, it thrives in rich, well drained soil in sunny rock gardens. Colours range from dark red, through pink, orange, yellow, cream, white and green.

Lachenalia (Cape cowslip): A South African lily with thick stems and delightful tubular flowers in the red, orange and yellow colour range. Flowering time is late winter to early spring. After the foliage has turned yellow it should be cut back, then the ground mulched with well-rotted compost. It prefers an open, sunny position.

*Divide bearded **iris** rhizomes with a clean, sharp knife.*

*Brilliant purple and yellow **iris**.*

Needs to be greenhouse or indoor potted cultivated in cool regions.

Leucojum (snowflake): A charming bulb for late winter, not to be confused with snowdrop (*Galanthus*). Growing to 45cm (18in) in height, the foliage is deep green and strap-like, while the small white bellflowers are tipped with green. Snowflakes will thrive in any moderately rich, free-draining soil and should be planted in either full sun or semi-shade.

Lilium (lily): Choose from the many hundreds of varieties of lily, ranging in height from 30cm (12in) to 2.5 metres (8ft), in a wide range of colours from pure white through cream, yellow, orange, pink, red, maroon, lilac and purple. The hardiness of lilies varies according to variety, so this should be checked with the nursery or plant supplier at the time of purchase. In general they will thrive if planted in full sun or semi-shade in deep, rich and well-drained soil.

Use a fork to lift bulbs after foliage has withered.

Muscari (grape hyacinth): Bulbs with dense heads of rich blue fragrant flowers are ideal for planting in borders and edges. Easy to cultivate in a wide range of soils and conditions, plant in full sun, as shade will increase leaf growth and reduce the quantity of flowers.

Narcissus (daffodil, jonquil): The most favoured and widely grown garden bulb, there are dozens of flower types, colours and forms. Ranging in size from 8cm (3in) to 45cm (18), both jonquils and daffodils can be grown with great success in a wide range of soils and conditions. However, their most important requirement is good drainage. Enrich the soil with plenty of organic matter before planting, or if growing at the base of trees, lightly mulch with well-rotted manure to improve the soil conditions.

Narcissus types:

1. Trumpet daffodils: large corona segment, one flower per stem.
2. Large-cupped daffodils: shorter corona,

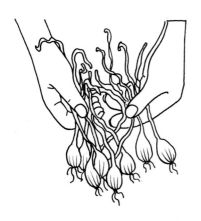

True bulbs are lifted and separated every few years to maintain healthy stocks.

Narcissus (daffodils) are the most popular and widely grown flowering bulbs.

one flower per stem.
3. Small-cupped daffodils: corona only one-third size of outer petals, single flower per stem.
4. Double daffodils: multiple corona segments, fluffy appearance. One flower per stem.
5. *Triandrus* hybrids: medium-size corona, several flowers to each stem.
6. *Cyclamineus* hybrids: one flower per stem, petals curved backwards.

Nerine (spider lily): A tall-growing bulb with slender stems topped by eight or more tubular flowers in autumn. Flowers range in colour from white to pink, orange and red according to species, they have a graceful spidery appearance. With the exception of **bowdenii**, these will require greenhouse cultivation in cooler regions. Bulbs exposed on the soil surface must be protected from frost. Avoid lifting bulbs for several years, instead, leave them to form a large established clump.

Primula vulgaris elatior (Polyanthus) : Although chiefly grown outdoors, they are also suitable for pot culture. Flowers up to 1.5" across, are carried in large trusses on stout stems above the leaves. For good results plant in an open, sunny position in rich, moist soil. Offsets can be replanted the following season.

Puschkinia scilloïdes (striped squill): A spring-flowering bulb with dainty pale blue or white star-like flowers, striped with darker blue on each petal. For the best results a cool climate is preferred, with

*Overleaf: **Endymion** (bluebells) used effectively as an edging plant.*

rich, moist soil with good drainage. Leave them undisturbed for several years until flowering diminishes, at which point they can be lifted and separated.

Ranunculus: A spring-flowering, tuberous-rooted bulb with tall stems of semi-double or double flowers from red through yellow and orange to cream, white, pink and multicolours. *Ranunculi* require plenty of water during the growing period; however it is important to let the soil dry out after the foliage has died back. Many gardeners actually dig up the roots at this stage and store them in a cool, dark and dry place until planting time the following season.

Scilla (squill): A cool climate bulb, which flowers in late winter and early spring. *Scilla* has strap-like foliage and stems of bellflowers that can be blue, violet, lilac, pink or white. Plant in full sun or semi-shade in deep, rich and well-drained soil, and mulch well after the foliage dies down.

Sparaxis (harlequin flower): A half-hardy and easy-to-grow corm with brightly coloured red, yellow, orange, pink, purple or white flowers in late spring. *Sparaxis* can be planted in autumn, in rich, well-drained soil, in a sheltered position in mild regions. Clumps can be left undisturbed for years, propagated by lifting and detaching cormlets and replanting. They will take two seasons to flower. *Sparaxis* is also suited to potting.

Sprekelia formosissima (Jacobean lily): A summer-flowering bulb with strap-like foliage and dramatic deep red flowers resembling orchids.

A cool greenhouse plant for cold regions, it may otherwise be planted in a sunny position in good, well-drained soil in autumn, water regularly and feed as foliage begins to emerge. They can be left in the ground for several years until flower production declines, then lift, separate and replant in autumn. Wait until foliage dies back before lifting.

Sternbergia: *Sternbergias* are fast growing, being planted in mid-summer and producing blooms in mid-autumn. The bright yellow flowers are on short stems and

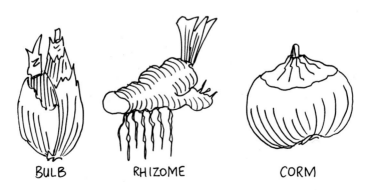

BULB   RHIZOME   CORM

True bulbs, rhizomes and corms.

Pretty **Ranunculus** *flower profusely during spring.*

resemble *crocus*. Each bulb produces one single flower. After flowering has finished the foliage continues to grow, eventually dying back in spring.

Do not cut back the foliage, but allow the cycle to complete.

Tulipa (tulip): Magnificent cold climate bulbs with many flower forms and colours from which to choose, ranging in height from 15cm (6in) to nearly one metre (3ft). Tulips can be grown in full sun or partial shade in rich, moist soil with good drainage. Sandy soil, which is slightly alkaline, suits them perfectly.

When the foliage turns yellow and starts to wither, the bulbs can be lifted for storage. Small offsets can be set on one side and replanted the next season, these may take two seasons before starting to flower.

Watsonia (bugle lily): A showy plant that makes an excellent high border, or it can be grown in clumps in a wild or cottage garden. It thrives in warm climates in deep, rich soil with adequate drainage. Suited to potted indoor cultivation in cool regions. Growing to 2 metres (6ft) when established, *watsonias* can be lavender, salmon, pink, orange, red and white in colour with strap-like leaves and tall flower spikes.

Zantedeschia (arum lily): A corm with broad, green, spear-shaped leaves and tall flower stems with elegant spathes instead of flowers. In a mild climate, well-drained, moist soil is essential, though plants can be positioned alongside streams or waterways with great success. Add plenty of organic matter to the soil prior to planting, then feed with a liquid fertiliser during early spring as the flowers form.

Well-established clumps can be divided in autumn. In cooler regions, they are best suited to potted tender greenhouse cultivation, but cope with placing outdoor during summer. Some varieties are suited to hardy aquatic cultivation, which are capable of winter survival in most regions.

INDEX